THE HUMAN BODY

THE LUNGS

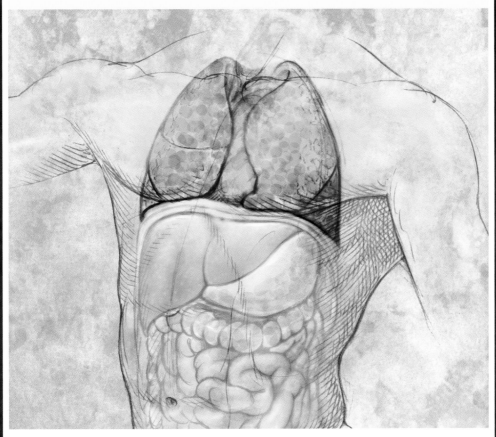

By Susan H. Gray

THE CHILD'S WORLD®
CHANHASSEN, MINNESOTA

The Child's World

Published in the United States of America by The Child's World®
PO Box 326, Chanhassen, MN 55317-0326
800-599-READ
www.childsworld.com

*Content Adviser:
R. John Solaro,
PhD, Distinguished
University Professor
Head, Department
of Physiology and
Biophysics, University
of Illinois at Chicago*

Photo Credits: Cover/frontispiece: Photodisc. Interior: Corbis: 12 (Lester V. Bergman), 18 (Bettmann), 25 (Layne Kennedy); Dr. John D. Cunningham/Visuals Unlimited: 15; Custom Medical Stock Photo: 9 (R. Lazarus), 16 (Hossler), 21 (L. Birmingham), 22 (P. Dennis); Getty Images/The Image Bank/Stuart Westmorland: 24; Getty Images/Stone: 11 (Yorgos Nika), 13 (Lori Adamski), 27 (John Millar); Getty Images/Taxi: 6 (Alistair Berg), 17 (FPG); PhotoEdit: 5 (David Young-Wolff), 7 (Park Street), 19 (Michael Newman), 23 (Dennis MacDonald).

The Child's World®: Mary Berendes, Publishing Director

Editorial Directions, Inc.: E. Russell Primm, Editorial Director; Pam Rosenberg, Editor; Katie Marsico, Associate Editor; Judith Shiffer, Assistant Editor; Matt Messbarger, Editorial Assistant; Susan Hindman, Copy Editor; Sarah E. De Capua, Proofreader; Judith Frisbie, Peter Garnham, Olivia Nellums, Chris Simms, Fact Checkers; Tim Griffin/IndexServ, Indexer; Cian Loughlin O'Day, Photo Researcher; Linda S. Koutris, Photo Editor

The Design Lab: Kathleen Petelinsek, Design; Kari Thornborough, Production Design

Library of Congress Cataloging-in-Publication Data
Gray, Susan Heinrichs.
  The lungs / by Susan H. Gray.
    p. cm. — (The human body)
  Includes index.
  ISBN 1-59296-428-1 (library bound : alk. paper) 1. Lungs—Juvenile literature. I. Title.
  QP121.G673 2005
  612.2—dc22   2005000573

TABLE OF CONTENTS

CHAPTER ONE

A THREAT THAT NEVER WORKS

Lisa was in a terrible mood. She kicked the sofa and shouted, "I'm going to hold my breath until you let me stay up late!" The babysitter just rolled her eyes. "Go ahead," she said. Lisa took a deep breath. She made an angry face and pinched her lips tight. The babysitter didn't even bother to watch.

Pretty soon, Lisa's eyes grew big. She knew she couldn't hold her breath much longer. What she didn't know was that carbon dioxide was building up in the cells of her body. Oxygen was running low as well. Her brain was sensing the problem. It was sending signals down to her chest muscles telling them to move so the girl could breathe. Finally, Lisa's muscles and lungs responded, and she let out a huge breath. "You win," she growled to the babysitter. Then she stomped off to bed.

Did you ever threaten to hold your breath until you got what you wanted? It didn't work because your brain sent signals to your lungs telling them to breathe.

CHAPTER TWO

WHAT ARE THE LUNGS?

The lungs are two large, pink, moist, spongy **organs** inside the chest. They expand every time we breathe in and shrink when we breathe out. These organs are made up of many tubes that lead to millions of tiny air pockets. But the lungs do much more than move air in and out of the chest. They work with the heart and blood vessels to deliver oxygen to cells throughout the body. They also help the cells to get rid of waste such as carbon dioxide.

Your lungs make it possible for you to blow out the candles on your birthday cake.

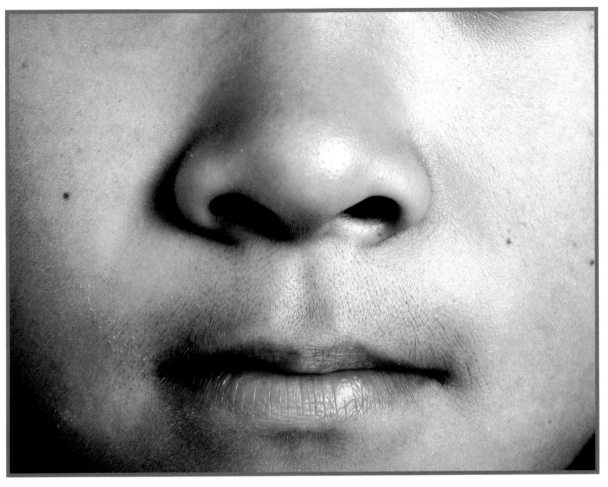

Did you know that your nose has important jobs to do? When you breathe in, your nose cleans and warms the air before it reaches your lungs.

When you inhale, or breathe in, air passes through your nose or mouth and into your throat. The nose warms, moistens, and filters the air. In the throat, the air passes through the voice box and into the windpipe, or trachea (TRAY-kee-uh). The bottom of the trachea splits into two branches. One branch goes into the left lung, and the other branch goes into the right. Each branch is called a bronchus (BRONK-us). Together, the two branches are called bronchi (BRONK-eye).

The two main bronchi split into smaller bronchi, then into very small branches called bronchioles (BRONK-ee-OLZ). Bronchioles divide into extremely small air passageways called alveolar (al-VEE-oh-lur) **ducts**. At the end of each duct is a cluster of air pockets. The cluster is called an alveolar sac, and each air pocket is called an alveolus (al-VEE-oh-luss).

Each alveolus is remarkably small and **delicate.** Its walls are made of single thin cells. Scientists estimate that, together, the two lungs contain about 300 million alveoli (al-VEE-oh-lye). If you could spread out the lungs so that all the alveoli were completely flat, they would cover an entire tennis court!

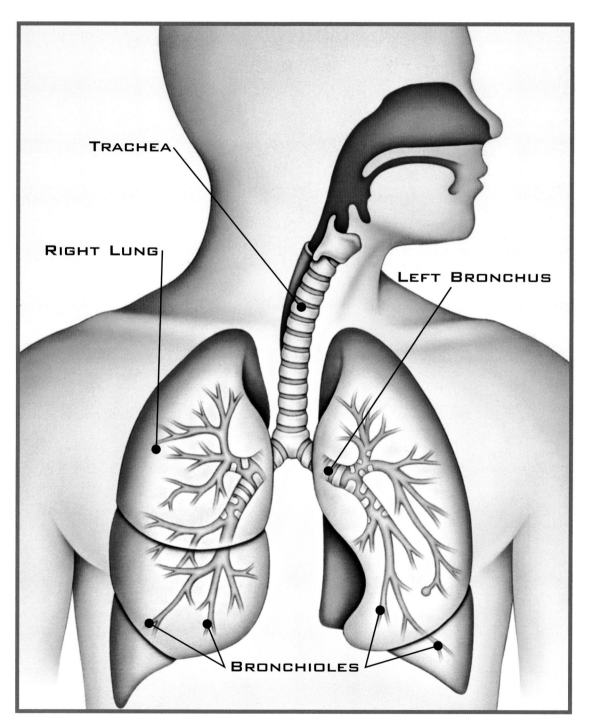

TRACHEA

RIGHT LUNG

LEFT BRONCHUS

BRONCHIOLES

If you could see inside your chest, your trachea and lungs would look something like this.

CHAPTER THREE

BLOOD EVERYWHERE

The lungs may be loaded with air passageways, ducts, and pockets, but this is only half the story. These organs are also jam-packed with vessels carrying blood. In fact, wherever there's lung tissue, there are blood vessels. Some vessels are as wide as your thumb. Some are only as thick as pencils, and some are so tiny you need a **microscope** to see them.

Two large blood vessels enter the lungs alongside the bronchi. These vessels carry blood straight from the heart to the lungs. Inside the lungs, the two big vessels divide and branch many times. The branches run alongside all of the air passageways. By the time they reach the alveoli, the vessels are quite small and narrow. The capillaries (KAP-ih-LEHR-eez) are the smallest of these vessels.

Blood is made up of red and white blood cells floating in fluid.

Once the blood cells enter the capillaries, they have traveled as deep

into the lungs as they can go. At this point, the blood starts to move

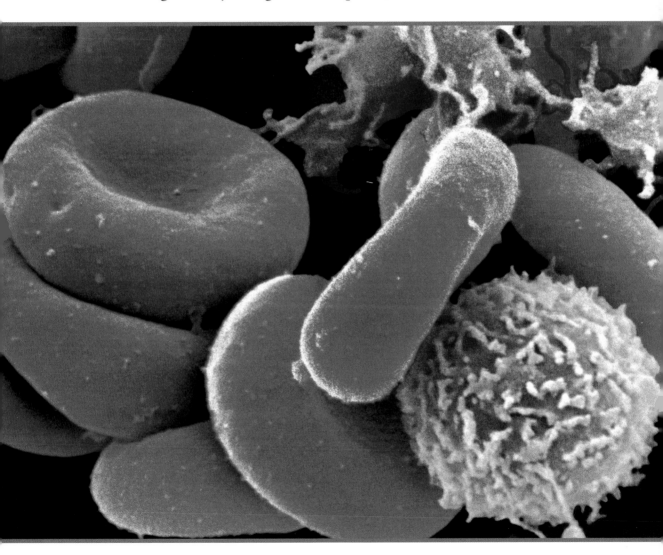

If you looked at your blood under a microscope, it would look like this. The red, doughnut-shaped cells are red blood cells.

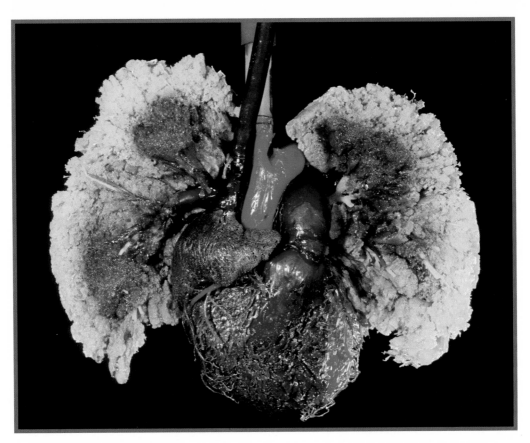

A model of the heart and lungs shows how the heart is positioned between the lungs.

back out. The capillaries join together to form bigger blood vessels, and the blood cells move into those. The vessels continue to join together until there are only two large vessels leaving the lungs. One leaves the left lung, and one leaves the right. Both vessels carry blood to the heart. The heart sits in a space between the two lungs, so blood does not have to travel far between the two organs.

CHAPTER FOUR

WHAT'S THE POINT?

Why do the lungs need all those blood vessels?

The lungs and blood work very closely together. They have two important jobs—to provide oxygen to every single cell in the body, and to haul away carbon dioxide.

Cells cannot live, work, or grow without oxygen. Muscles can't move, eyes can't see, and brains can't think unless their cells are getting a constant supply. As they work, cells produce a waste gas called carbon dioxide. Red

When you exercise, your muscles need a lot of oxygen to keep working properly. So your heart beats faster to get oxygen-rich blood flowing more quickly through your body.

cells in the blood deliver oxygen **molecules** and haul away carbon

dioxide molecules.

Here's how it works: The blood is in constant motion. Every time

the heart beats, it pumps out blood through large blood vessels. As

these vessels get farther from the heart, they branch and become

narrower. Blood travels through smaller and smaller vessels until it

reaches the smallest ones of all—the capillaries.

Capillaries are everywhere—in the deepest muscles, just under the

fingernails, and even inside the heart itself. They are in touch with just

about every cell in the body. When red blood cells scoot through the

capillaries, they release oxygen molecules to all the other cells nearby.

They also pick up carbon dioxide molecules. Once they've traded out

these molecules, the blood cells start moving back to the heart. They

travel through larger and larger vessels until they reach it.

Next, the heart pumps that blood to the lungs. The blood

again moves through large vessels and eventually flows into the

lungs. It travels farther and farther until it enters the capillaries

around the alveoli. This time, as they scoot through the capillaries,

the blood cells give up their carbon dioxide molecules. The waste

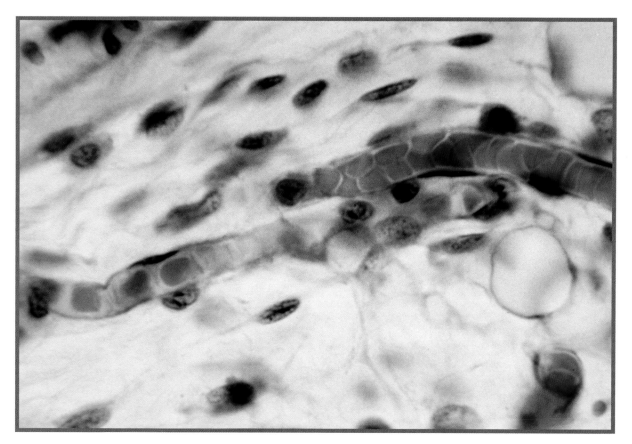

The walls of capillaries are made up of a single layer of cells. They are so tiny that blood cells must line up in single file to pass through them.

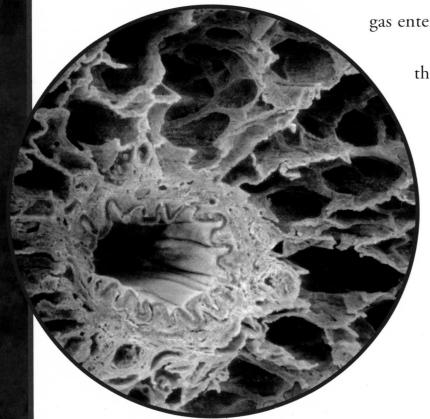

gas enters the alveoli. While the cells are still in the capillaries, they receive oxygen molecules from the alveoli. The blood moves on, loaded with oxygen and cleared

A bronchiole is surrounded by dozens of alveoli.

of carbon dioxide. It goes back to the heart and is again pumped out to the body. In this way, cells everywhere keep getting the oxygen they need. And they get rid of waste before it builds up. Clearly, the lungs and blood could not do their jobs without each other.

Doctors and scientists have known for centuries that the heart and lungs worked together. But they often had strange ideas about how this took place.

From early on, doctors were aware that the heart was a beating organ. They also knew that the lungs were soft, spongy organs that surrounded and overlapped the heart. About 2,000 years ago, a Greek doctor named Galen thought that the lungs existed to cool the heart and keep it from overheating.

This idea persisted for centuries. Even in the late 1100s, a doctor wrote that the lungs' job was to "withstand the warmth of the heart" and keep it cool. Years later, doctors went a step further. They said that the lungs actually controlled people's feelings. For example, if someone was angry, people believed that cool air from the lungs would calm that person down.

In the 1400s, the great artist and scientist Leonardo da Vinci (below) formed his own ideas about the lungs. He said that

impure air, or "sooty vapors," traveled from the heart to the lungs. He believed these bad gases left the body when a person exhaled, or breathed out. Da Vinci did not know exactly how this happened, but at least he was on the right track.

In 1628, a famous doctor named William Harvey began to figure out the real relationship between the heart and lungs. He said that the lungs were made up of many passageways and air spaces. He also said that blood traveled through the lungs.

Harvey did not know about capillaries, but he reasoned that such vessels probably existed. His ideas proved to be correct. In 1661, scientist Marcello Malpighi (left) discovered capillaries and the tiny blood cells that move through them. With this new knowledge, scientists finally realized that the lungs were much more than just a couple of cool organs.

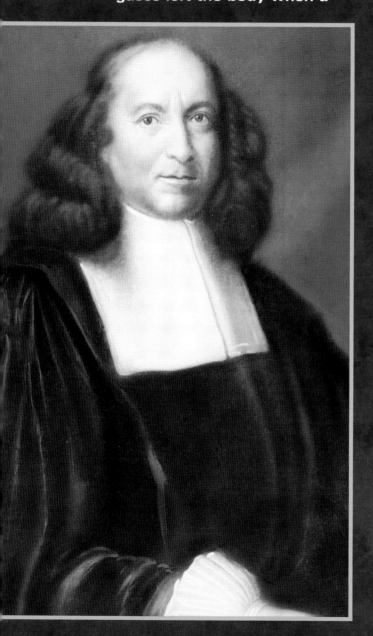

CHAPTER FIVE

ARE ANY OTHER STRUCTURES INVOLVED?

When you inhale and exhale, the lungs are not the only structures at work. Muscles, bones, and nerves also play important roles.

The main muscle involved is the diaphragm (DY-uh-fram). It is a big sheet of muscle that forms a floor under the lungs. The lungs and heart are just above it, and the stomach lies below it. When the diaphragm is relaxed, it is dome shaped. As it contracts, it flattens down. The lungs then

Take a deep breath. Can you feel your muscles and bones moving to make room for your air-filled lungs?

expand to fit into the larger space. This is what happens when you inhale.

As the diaphragm contracts, little muscles between the ribs also contract. They pull the ribs up and out, causing the chest to swell. After a second or two, the diaphragm and rib muscles relax. The diaphragm returns to its dome shape, and the ribs drop back down. The lungs shrink, forcing air out and causing you to exhale.

When your body's muscles contract and your bones move, it's often because you are controlling them. You make them move on purpose. But the muscles and bones involved in breathing are a little different. You don't always move them on purpose. In fact, you usually don't even think about them.

This is because nerves from the brain take care of things. A section of the brain called the brain stem controls important activities that we

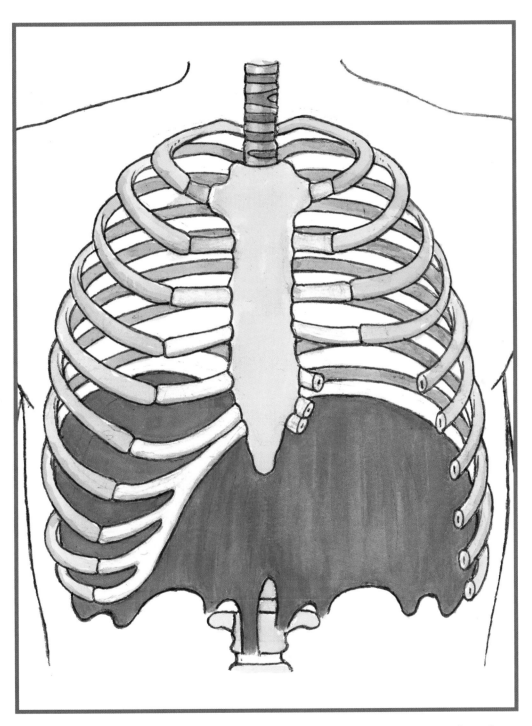

When you inhale and exhale, your diaphragm and rib cage have important jobs to do.

are not usually aware of. Such activities include the beating of the heart and breathing. Electrical signals that control breathing leave the brain stem. They travel along nerves to the diaphragm and rib muscles. The signals cause the muscles to contract.

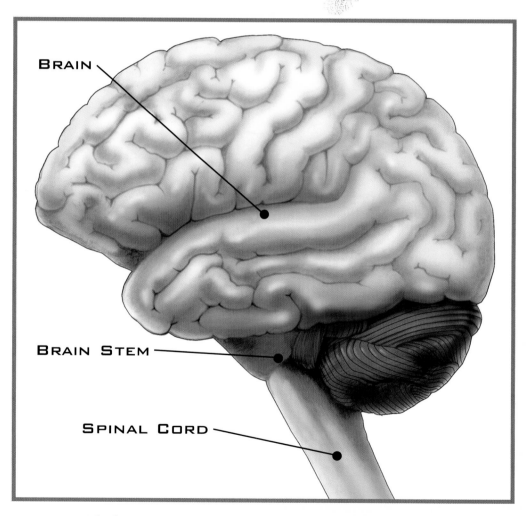

The brain stem connects the spinal cord with the rest of the brain.

*You can hold your breath when you want to swim underwater,
but only for a short time. Soon you will need to come up for air.*

You can **override** those brain signals by controlling your

breathing on purpose. For example, you can hold your breath when

you swim underwater. But you can't override the signals for long.

The brain detects when there's too much carbon dioxide in the

blood and sends out signals that force you to breathe.

Have you ever wondered how a fish breathes underwater? After all, it needs to take in oxygen and get rid of carbon dioxide just like humans do. To accomplish this, fish use their gills.

Gills are the bright red structures on the sides of a fish's head. They are usually hidden from view by some kind of covering or flap. Gills are very delicate and are loaded with blood vessels. The constant flow of blood gives gills their red color.

As a fish swims, water passes over its gills. Oxygen in the water seeps into the gills' blood vessels, and carbon dioxide in the blood seeps out. Gills are so delicate that they collapse when a fish is removed from the water. In this collapsed state, gills cannot draw oxygen from the air or release carbon dioxide.

One fish is an exception. The walking catfish (above) has especially stiff gills. They do not collapse quickly if the fish is removed from the water. This unusual feature makes it possible for the catfish to come up on land for short periods of time and breathe the air. The catfish drags itself along by "walking" with its whiskers and wiggling back and forth. It cannot travel very far this way, but it's often able to move from one body of water to another.

CHAPTER SIX

WHAT'S NEW WITH THE LUNGS?

Today, scientists continue to study how the lungs work. Some are trying to figure out what causes asthma (AZ-muh). This is a disorder in which the bronchi and bronchioles close down. People with asthma often gasp for air until their passageways open up again. Scientists are trying to learn how tobacco smoke, dust, and pollen affect these individuals.

Other scientists are studying the ways that smoking harms the lungs. They have found that there are more than 3,000 chemicals in cigarette smoke and that many of these cause disease.

Although scientists know a lot about the lungs, they also realize that there's plenty more to learn about these incredible organs.